Contents

Caterpillar Cake 4

Skim 6

Little Boat 7

Let's Go! 8

Zany Zoo 10

When I Swing 12

Hide and Seek 14

School Photo 16

This Little Pencil 18

Feeling Sniffy 19

On the Carpet 20

Here It Comes 22

My Shell 24

Kitty Cat 26

Bathtime 27

River Lullaby 28

Caterpillar Cake

caterpillar
caterpillar
caterpillar cake

it's the only thing
that my mum can make

crunchy
crispy
juicy too

filled with
caterpillar goo!

Skim

I love to skim a pebble
when I'm playing at the beach

I throw it out as far
as my arm can reach

I watch it skipping smoothly
on the surface of the sea

skim little pebble

go **1**
2
3!

Little Boat

little boat
on the sea
bobs about
waves at me

yellow sail
silver sway
little boat
drifts
    away

Let's Go!

Let's go!
Let's go!
I am first
in the race!

Let's go!
Let's go!
Blasting straight
into space!

Let's go!
Let's go!
In my fine
rocket ship!

Let's go!
Let's go!
What a trip!
What a trip!

Zany Zoo

At the zany zoo
I could see:

5 crazy crocodiles

4 slippery snakes

3 tough tigers

2 moody monkeys

and **1** fat frog

When I Swing

When I swing
I seem
to forget
everything,

I wash
my mind
in the sky.

Feet first
I burst
this blur
of world

and

fly

fly

fly.

12

Hide and Seek

hide in the butter
hide in a tree
hide in the nest
of a big bumblebee

hide in a teapot
hide in a drawer
hide in the teeth
of a crocodile's jaw

hide in a slipper
hide in a shoe
hide in a bottle
of PVA glue

hide in a mattress
hide in the sink
hide in the fizz
of your big brother's drink

hide in a beanbag
hide in a pram
hide in a jar
of raspberry jam

hide in the flannel
hide in the snow
I can still find you
wherever you go

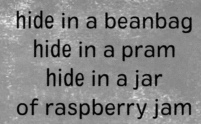

School Photo

brush hair
wash face
pack bag
tie lace

give mum
big hug
don't step
in mud

walk quick
on time
at school
all fine

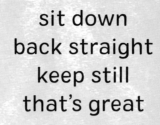

sit down
back straight
keep still
that's great

teeth white
hands link
big smile

now... **BLINK!**

This Little Pencil

This little pencil
     drew a little l i n e
         dabbed a little dot
    shaped a little squiggle
         didn't wanna stop

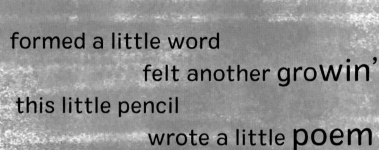

    formed a little word
        felt another growin'
   this little pencil
        wrote a little poem

I Love Poetry!

Feeling Sniffy

Dandelion seeds are f l y i n g
f r e e upon the breeze.

They're so pretty, it's a pity
that they make me sneeze!

On The Carpet

on the carpet
    sit up straight

on the carpet
    feeling great

on the carpet
    listen, learn

on the carpet
    take a turn

on the carpet
    story time

on the carpet
    words and rhyme

on the carpet
    let's do maths

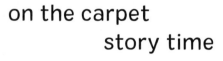

on the carpet
lots of laughs

on the carpet
we don't moan

off the carpet
all go home

Here It Comes

snuggle down
snow's in town
dressing gown
bed

morning light
snowball fight
shining bright
sled

22

My Shell

there is a shell
alone on a beach
over the sand-dunes
out of my reach

it calls to me softly
whispers my name
says, 'come, won't you find me?'
always the same

one day I will see it
half-buried in sand
and hold it up proud
in the palm of my hand

we'll sing of the sun
and the salt and the sea
together forever
just my shell and me

25

Kitty Cat

pretty cat, oh
kitty cat, oh
skitty little city cat, oh
pretty cat, oh
kitty cat, oh
won't you sit with me?

furry cat, oh
purry cat, oh
hurly-burly early cat, oh
furry cat, oh
purry cat, oh
curled up on my knee.

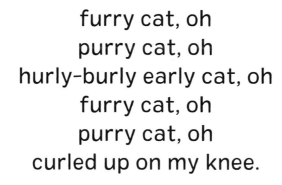

Bathtime

It's a bit of a laugh, in the bath –

there's **bubbles** and **squeaks**
when I slide on both cheeks

playing with **toys**
and making a noise

wrinkly **skin**
and shampoo on the chin

there's **dancing** about
when it's time to get out.

It's a bit of a laugh, in the bath!

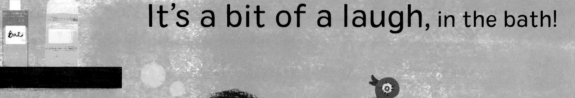

River Lullaby

Sliding through the silence of high night peaks
hush little shush little
rush little river

Swallowing secrets that the moon-child speaks
hush little shush little
rush little river

Furrowing fields as a dark frost creeps
hush little shush little
rush little river

Silver-line dreams where cityscapes sleep
hush little shush little
rush little river

Rumble ever onwards – it's a journey to be free
hush little shush little
rush little river

Back into the arms of a dawn-dressed sea
hush little shush little
shush little river

For Roman and Oscar, with love – K.P–S.

For Leo, Clement and Ignatius – M.G.